GLACIERS

Michael George

CREATIVE EDITIONS

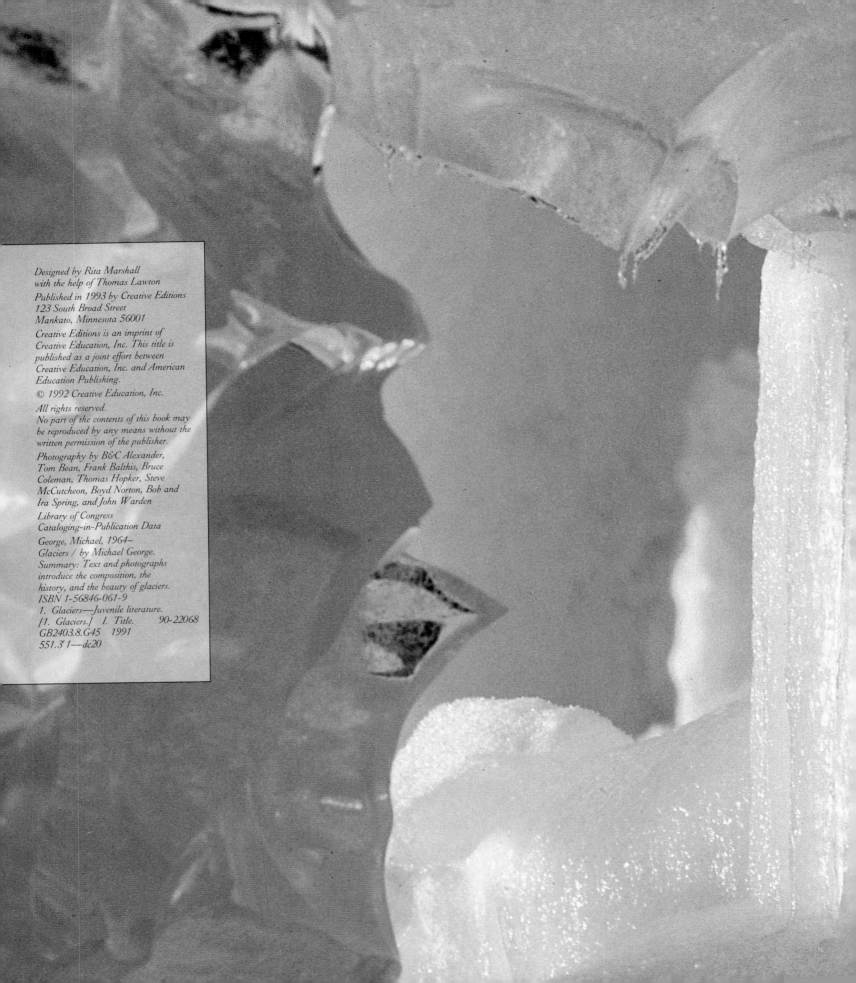

Designed by Rita Marshall
with the help of Thomas Lawton

Published in 1993 by Creative Editions
123 South Broad Street
Mankato, Minnesota 56001

Creative Editions is an imprint of
Creative Education, Inc. This title is
published as a joint effort between
Creative Education, Inc. and American
Education Publishing.

Photography by B&C Alexander,
Tom Bean, Frank Balthis, Bruce
Coleman, Thomas Hopker, Steve
McCutcheon, Boyd Norton, Bob and
Ira Spring, and John Warden

Library of Congress
Cataloging-in-Publication Data

George, Michael, 1964–
Glaciers / by Michael George.
Summary: Text and photographs
introduce the composition, the
history, and the beauty of glaciers.
ISBN 1-56846-061-9
1. Glaciers—Juvenile literature.
[1. Glaciers.] I. Title.   90-22068
GB2403.8.G45 1991
551.3′1—dc20

In Memory of
George R. Peterson, Sr.

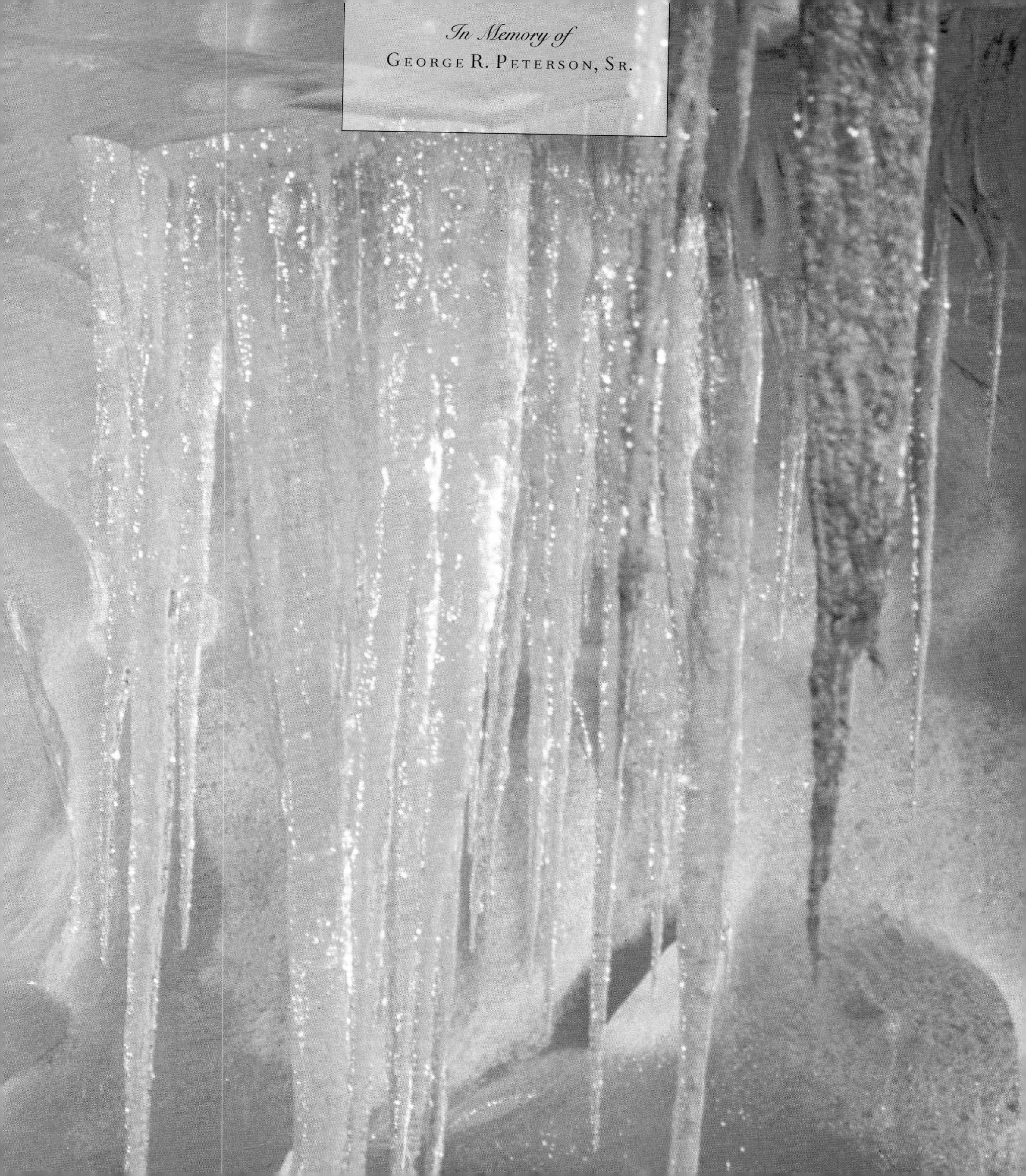

7

Glaciers are thick, flowing rivers of ice. Their size is imposing and their progress un-yielding. Over millions of years, they have gradually sculpted the jagged mountains and steep-sided valleys that beautify the Earth. Still carving the landscape today, *Glaciers* are often more spectacular than the stunning scenery they create. In the future they may advance to cover the Earth's land, or they may melt to flood the world's coasts. In either case, glaciers will continue to reveal the power and beauty of nature.

An iceberg.

Glaciers are born in cold climates, where frequent storms blanket the earth with white, fluffy snow. The *Snowflakes* that cover the ground come in a variety of forms, including icy needles, dusty powder, and six-sided crystals. After a time, snowflakes on the ground lose their lacy shapes and join together into tiny balls of ice. These grains of snow can be seen in dirty snowdrifts, or on the side of the road on a spring day.

As the days of spring grow gradually warmer, the Sun's rays melt the Earth's blanket of snow. In some areas, however, temperatures never rise high enough to melt the grains of snow. In polar regions and atop high mountains, fresh snow piles up year after year, burying older grains of snow

Snow blankets the ground.

under a thick, heavy layer of insulation. The tremendous weight compresses the grains of snow and they fuse together. Eventually, pockets of air that surround the grains are even forced out. What was once a covering of soft, white snow becomes a slab of hard, *Blue Ice.*

As the years pass, snow continues to accumulate and the slab of ice grows steadily thicker. Eventually, the slab of ice becomes too massive to sit peacefully still. Just as gravity pulls a skier down a ski slope, gravity pulls the ice down the mountain. Once the ice begins to move, it is called a glacier.

Blue ice.

A glacier follows the path of existing valleys like a slow-flowing river of ice. The speed that a glacier moves depends on the thickness of the ice and on the steepness of the slope. The fastest glaciers are hundreds of feet thick and flow down steep mountains. Temperature also affects a glacier's speed. Glaciers move most quickly when temperatures are warm, because they slide on a thin, slippery layer of water. The distance that most glaciers move in a day ranges from several inches to several feet. However, the fastest glaciers cover over one hundred feet a day.

A glacier.

Surprisingly, all parts of a glacier do not move at the same speed. This fact is easily observed by placing stakes across the width of a glacier. After a time, the stakes in the middle are farther downhill than those near the edges, revealing that the middle of a glacier moves faster than its edges. A glacier's various layers also move at different speeds. Metal pipes drilled deep into glaciers eventually bend, showing that the surface moves faster than deeper layers. This is because the layers of ice nearest the Earth are slowed by the underlying terrain.

Glaciers move at different speeds.

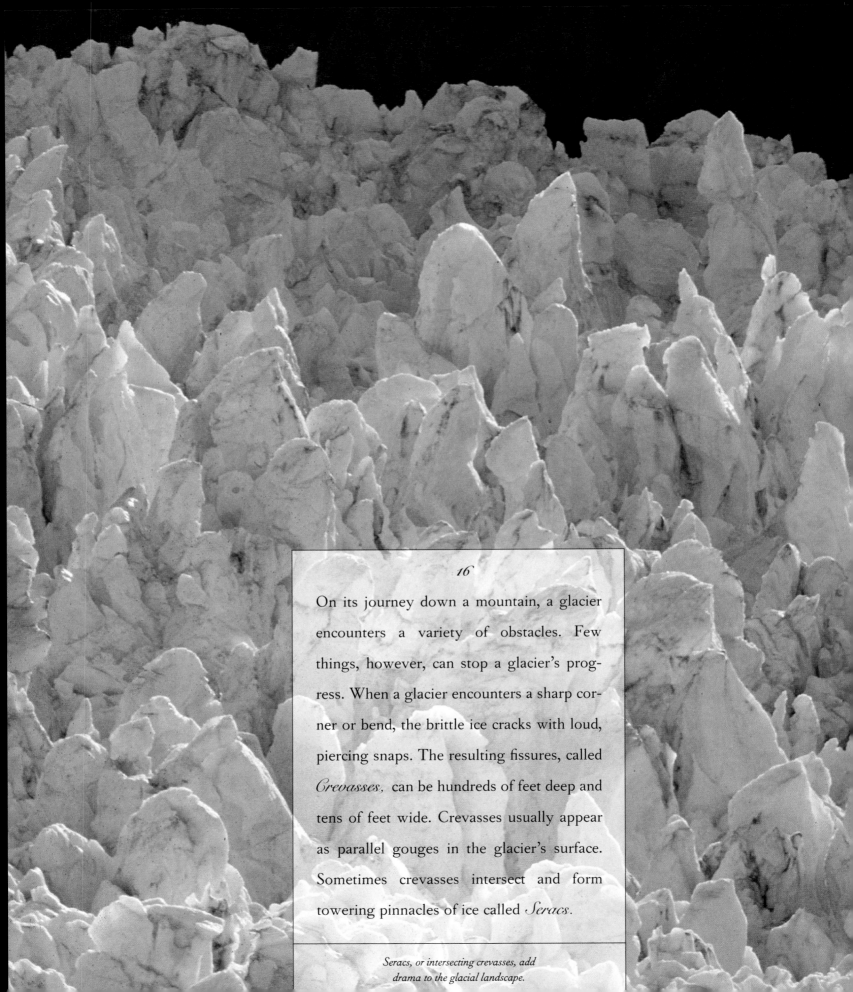

16

On its journey down a mountain, a glacier encounters a variety of obstacles. Few things, however, can stop a glacier's progress. When a glacier encounters a sharp corner or bend, the brittle ice cracks with loud, piercing snaps. The resulting fissures, called *Crevasses,* can be hundreds of feet deep and tens of feet wide. Crevasses usually appear as parallel gouges in the glacier's surface. Sometimes crevasses intersect and form towering pinnacles of ice called *Seracs.*

*Seracs, or intersecting crevasses, add
drama to the glacial landscape.*

19

As a glacier weaves its way downhill, the ice flows over underlying rocks. Ice has an adhesive grip, which you can feel if you touch a cold ice cube tray with damp hands. Because of this grip, rocks stick to glaciers and give the ice tremendous powers of erosion. Like a giant file, the flowing rocks and ice grate the underlying terrain. Atop high peaks, where glaciers are born and nourished with falling snow, the glacial ice gouges mountainsides into bowl-shaped hollows, called *Cirques.* Where two glaciers occupy valleys that lie side by side, they produce a sharp, jagged ridge known as an *Arete.* Occasionally, a mountain peak is completely surrounded by glaciers. Over many years, the glaciers eat into the mountain, carving the peak into a pointed, pyramid-shaped horn.

A cirque.
Inset: An arete separates two glaciers.

Farther down the mountain, a glacier plows through rock, soil, and vegetation like a gigantic bulldozer, carving the V-shaped valleys cut by rivers into steep-sided, U-shaped troughs. The material scraped from the Earth dirties the clean, white surface of the glacier. Most of this rocky debris is pushed aside, and piles up along the edges of the glacier. The rest is carried all the way to the glacier's base, where it is finally dumped. The resulting pile of material, a *Moraine*, contains rock and soil in a variety of forms: from unworn, massive boulders to finely grated silt.

Moraines build up along glaciers.

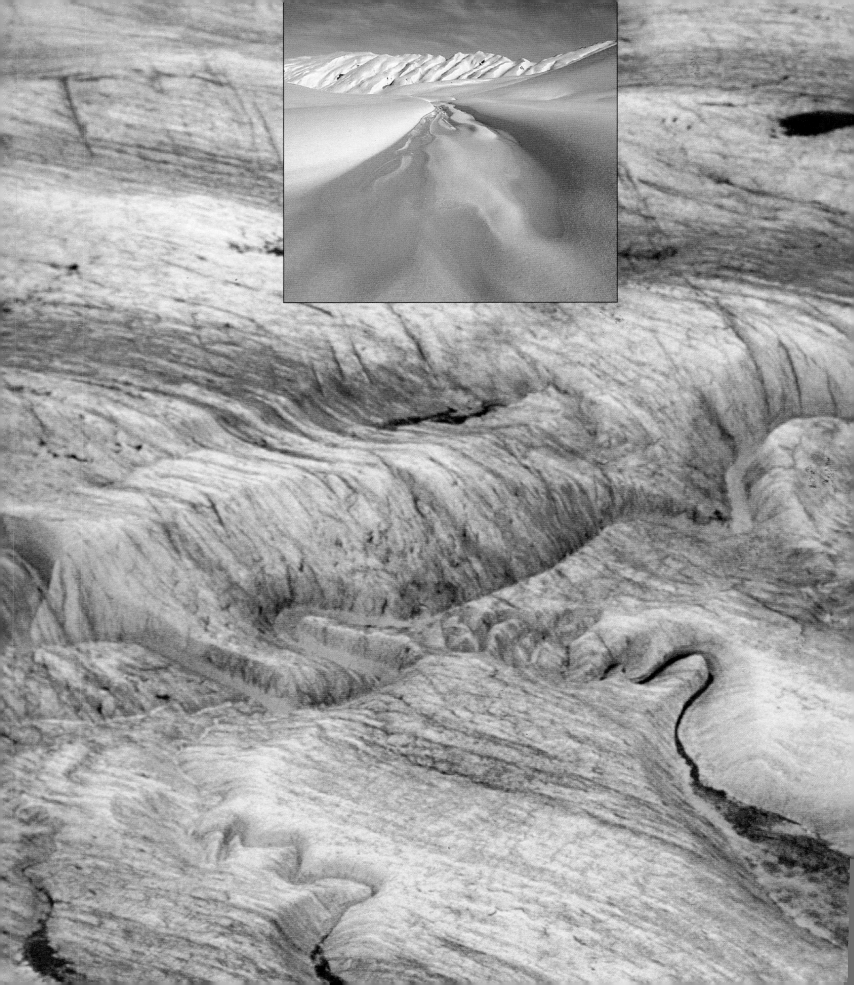

Glaciers are awesome instruments of erosion, relentlessly plowing through the Earth and its vegetation. A glacier's forward progress, however, can be stopped by two equally mighty forces. One of these is heat. When the bone-chilling days of winter are replaced by the mild days of spring, warm winds and sunshine soften the surface of the glacier. The glacier glistens with moisture as streams of *Meltwater* wear channels, tunnels, and caves in the ice.

Although the glacier continues to flow downhill, warm temperatures completely melt the flowing ice at its base. As a result, the glacier may actually stop its forward progress, or may even melt backward up the mountain. Eventually, the base stops its retreat where summer temperatures remain below freezing. Here the glacier waits for winter, when cold temperatures allow it to advance once again.

Sunshine makes meltwater.
Inset: Warmth softens a glacier.

In some regions, summer temperatures are not warm enough to stop a glacier's forward progress. Instead, perpetually cold temperatures enable the rivers of ice to flow all the way to the ocean. The sea, however, is as potent an adversary as the warm summer sun; it is the second mighty force that can halt a glacier. Wherever glaciers meet the coast, enormous *Ice Shelves* extend over the water, towering hundreds of feet above the surface. Waves smash against the ice, causing massive chunks to break off and crash into the ocean. This process is called *Calving*, and the masses of ice which float out to sea are called *Icebergs*. Once freed from land, icebergs float toward warmer climates. Gradually, the Sun's rays melt the islands of ice.

Ice calving from a glacier.
Inset: Floating icebergs.

Polar seas, such as the North Atlantic, are often littered with thousands of icebergs. These icebergs are calved from ice sheets, enormous layers of ice and snow that have completely buried polar land masses. With only the sea to stop their spread, ice sheets produce most of the world's icebergs.

❧

There are only two ice sheets on the Earth's surfaces: one in Antarctica and the other in Greenland. The Greenland ice sheet covers 670,000 square miles and is almost two miles thick at its center. Many times larger than the Greenland ice sheet, the Antarctic ice sheet covers more than 5 million square miles—an area larger than the United States, Mexico, and Central America put together. Two and a half miles thick at its center, the Antarctic ice sheet hides entire

Icebergs in the polar seas.

mountain ranges beneath its surface. This enormous layer of ice accounts for 90 percent of all the ice in the world and contains more water than all the Earth's rivers and lakes combined.

Although the Greenland and Antarctic ice sheets seem enormous, they are small when compared to the ice sheets that existed long ago. Thousands of years ago the Earth's climate was cooler than it is today, and ice sheets covered much of the land. In fact, ice sheets have advanced several times in the history of the Earth. Each period of ice advance, called an *Ice Age* or a glacial, is followed by a period when temperatures warm and the ice retreats to the cold polar regions of the globe. The warm climate we enjoy today caused the latest retreat of the ice sheets.

The face of a glacier in Antarctica.

Although twelve thousand years have passed since the last ice age, ancient glaciers left lasting imprints on the Earth's surface, just as modern glaciers do today. Ancient glaciers are responsible for the cirques, aretes, and U-shaped valleys that decorate many mountainsides. Small valleys often hang high above the floor of the largest U-shaped valleys. These hanging valleys were carved by small tributary glaciers that combined with larger, more powerful glaciers.

A U-shaped valley in Alaska.

33

There is also evidence of past ice ages on level land. As the glaciers advanced, finely ground silt polished smooth the underlying bedrock. At the same time, jagged rocks stuck in the ice gouged deep scratches across the smoothened bedrock. In northern regions these scrapes can still be seen, along with the rounded boulders and moraines that the glaciers deposited.

Bedrock scored by glaciers.
Inset: Glacial erratics.

Ancient glaciers are also responsible for the stunning scenery along some coasts. During past glacials, the enormous ice sheets that covered the globe tied up much of the Earth's water. As a result, sea levels were much lower than they are today. Naturally, glaciers descended to the former sea level, carving their characteristic steep-sided valleys. As the climate warmed, the ice sheets melted and sea levels rose, filling the valleys with water. Today, these submerged valleys, called *Fiords*, indent the coasts of many regions. The most spectacular fiords are found along the coast of Norway.

A glacial fiord.

The Earth's landscape reveals abundant evidence of past ice ages. Only recently, however, did scientists come up with an adequate explanation for past glacials. Most scientists now believe that ice ages are caused by variations in the Earth's orbit around the Sun. Periodically, the Earth moves farther from the Sun. As a result, the amount of heat we receive from the Sun decreases, the Earth's climate cools, and the ice sheets advance.

In the past, periods of warmer climate and retreating ice have lasted about ten thousand years. Since the current period of retreating ice has already lasted twelve thousand years, some scientists believe another period of *Glaciation* is long overdue. However, human activities may postpone this expected ice age. By destroying forests and burning

Front edge of an ice sheet.

fossil fuels, humankind increases the amount of carbon dioxide in the atmosphere. The additional carbon dioxide traps the Sun's heat, something like a blanket. Therefore, instead of a gradual cooling, there may be a gradual warming of the Earth's climate.

Although a warmer climate seems preferable, it may not necessarily be better than a colder one. Significantly warmer temperatures could melt much of the world's ice, and the results might be disastrous. If the world's glaciers and ice sheets melted, sea levels would rise over two hundred feet and flood vast areas of the Earth. Cities such as London and Paris would be under water, along with entire countries such as Denmark and the Netherlands.

Many shapes of icebergs.

40

Whether the *Glaciers* retreat or advance, human civilization and the world environment are intimately related to these relentless rivers of ice. Although they are formed by delicate snowflakes, glaciers grow to imposing sizes, and build awesome strength. They challenge the bravest explorers, sculpt jagged mountain peaks, and carve coastal fiords. Whether they flood the world with water or cover the land with ice, glaciers embody the power and beauty of nature.

Powerful glaciers.